Joanie Boney Books

www.joanieboneybooks.com

About the Author:
Joanie Boney books
are multicultural and
multiracial reflecting the
true America.

BroMiguel Illustrations at EstudioEdge.com

Thank you for purchasing a Joanie Boney Book:)

My mom and dad bought me
a new car for being good.

My car is just like Dad's car.

They told me that I must take good care of it.

My car makes noises just
like my dad's car.

Its red.

My car has tinted windows just like Dad's car.

Mom and Dad bought me new sun glasses to wear in my car.

Big wheels just like Dads car.

It even has air conditioning just like Dad's.

My car has a radio just like Dad's car.

Mom bought me a new hat
to wear in my car.

I like singing in my car just like Dad does.

I like eating in my car just like Dad.

I like drinking my favorite juice in my car just like Dad.

I like washing my car on the
drive-way just like Dad.

I like driving my car to the park just like Dad.

Sometimes my friends and I drive
down the sidewalk in my car.

Sometimes we all just hang out in my car.

I love my new car, don't you?

Thanks, Mom and Dad, for my new car!

www.ingramcontent.com/pod-product-compliance
Lightning Source LLC
Chambersburg PA
CBHW041243040426
42445CB00004B/128